SEPTEMBER 26, 1940

The Ligne à Grande Vitesse (LGV) line from Perpignan to Figueres is due to open in February 2009.

The 44.4 km line, which includes an 8.3 km tunnel bored through the Pyrenees, under the Col de Perthus (the principal route through the mountains since antiquity), will ultimately slash travel times between Paris and Barcelona and in doing so also will render one of the infrastructural follies of the pre–European Union days obsolete.

The marshalling yards at the Portbou railway station are a sprawling mass of sidings that take up around a third of this small town. A monastic fishing port since the tenth century, for most of the twentieth century Portbou existed as a kind of enforced caesura in the flow of European traffic, partly by dint of being a busy customs point between France and Spain, but mainly because the railway lines installed by the Spanish government in the 1870s were of incompatible gauge with the French tracks running through its counterpart border town of Cerbère. Travellers entering or leaving Spain would be forced to wait for hours whilst the wheelbase of their train was changed to accommodate this difference in gauge.

Around 60% of the world's rail lines follow George Stephenson's Standard gauge (4' 8 ½" or 1,435 mm) — based originally on the width of the horse-drawn fixed rail lines of the Northern English collieries in the early nineteenth century (though there are persistent apocryphal claims that the standardised width was derived from the traces of wagon ruts from pre-existing Roman roads in the region). The remaining 40% of rail lines are of varying width from country to country or from economic region to region. For example, the celebrated engineer Isambard Kingdom Brunel argued strongly in favour of his 7' ¼" or 2,140 mm Broad gauge, and it ran for a sustained period on the Great Western Line in England, whilst in Ireland the gauge width of 5' 3" or 1,600 mm was said to be a compromise between Broad and Standard gauges – an imprudent decision that had long-reaching effects until Ireland's economic resurgence in the 1990s. In the U.S., the North-East ran on Standard gauge due to its early carriages being imported from Great Britain, whilst the South ran on Broad gauge until the Reconstruction era after the American Civil War.

In Spain, the lines rolling into Portbou are Indian gauge (5' 6" or 1,676 mm) – a width first adopted in Canada in the 1830s and still the most popular commercial gauge in the world (largely due to its use throughout India and Pakistan, as well as Spain, Argentina and Chile). Arriving into the town, they converge with the Standard gauge lines from France, interspersed with mixed gauge lines installed for transitions, the whole ensemble wedged onto a natural steppe set into the Albère foothills.

Like the sidings, Portbou Station and its huge customs house seem disproportionately large for their surroundings. Built in 1929, in time for Barcelona's International Expo, the station and custom house buildings would survive Catalonia's suppression under Franco, and the intrigues and repression of the Second World War (during which time the Gestapo frequented the town despite Spain's ostensible neutrality), but they cannot survive the imperatives of the European Union and the constant demands of standardisation in a globalising economy. The customs house was the first to be affected, following Spain's joining of the European Community in 1986 and ratification of the Maastricht Treaty in 1992. The border, which had been actively controlled since the 1659 Treaty of the Pyrenees, was now downgraded to a largely symbolic boundary (barring a short period when heavy French taxes ensured a flow of French pastis drinkers into the bars and wine stores of their neighbour). In 2009, the LGV line will deliver the same obsolescent status to the railway station, as the mean speed at which travellers encounter the town changes permanently.

It is a moment that has perhaps forced the town to reassess its ambivalent relationship with another key point in its history — the overnight internment and death of the critic and philosopher Walter Benjamin on the evening of September 26, 1940.

Benjamin had arrived in Portbou following a harrowing walk from Banyuls-sur-Mer, having fatally mistimed his attempt to flee the Nazis. Stopped by a police patrol in Portbou, he was found to have the correct papers for his ongoing journey to Lisbon and, ultimately, New York, but to have the incorrect papers for leaving France. He was placed overnight in La Fonda França Inn (owned by a Franco sympathiser), due to be returned to the French authorities the next day. Following the ruling of a treaty signed just two days earlier, they would in turn have been compelled to hand him straight over to the Gestapo. Some controversy exists about the exact sequence of events that followed but — whether through exhaustion, morphine-induced suicide or murder — Benjamin was dead by the following morning.

At the time of this writing, Benjamin's death is marked in the town by a series of street signs in four languages, an elegant cliffside monument by artist Dani Karavan and a prominent grave that may or may not contain Benjamin's remains. The grave quietly bears witness to the visits of occasional pilgrims and is discreetly adorned with earnest notes, cairns and photographs — with the effect being less Jim Morrison than anonymous ad hoc roadside shrine. The few street signs for tourists bear other marks — graffiti written by local separatists, bullet holes and the occasional swastika, as well as the international language of delinquent teenage scribbling. A few waterside restaurants run along a spur just to the side of the tourist booth (sitting like a vestigial sentry post on a hairpin bend in the main road to France). None of the restaurants directly references

Benjamin yet. Most of the owners and staff are old enough to have been witnesses of or even party to the conspiracies of silence that marked the Franco years and a few will have lived through the Second World War years too. They would perhaps prefer that the clock could be turned back to the heyday of the railway and its supply of captive diners, rather than the town relying on a death during one of its most ignominious hours.

Yet looking at the potential oxbow lake syndrome that faces Portbou, that hope looks like the best chance of the town thriving in that future. The LGV is now routinely being compared not with the tortuous rail journey that it replaces but against the times offered by budget airlines that might link, for instance, Marseilles to Barcelona. On the Spanish side, the line will run from Figueres — a town that has had none of Portbou's ambivalence about its own association with Salvador Dali, spawning a 'celebrity-industry' that is predicted to go from strength to strength as the key cultural attraction in the region. In infrastructural terms, the Portbou marshalling yards are not just being replaced; their presence and comparative relevance is being effaced from the popular accounts of desirable movement in the region.

Ironically, the paper-filled suitcase that contemporary reports had Benjamin guarding jealously during his last days was said to have been removed to Figueres, where it was supposedly kept in an archive until 1975, when it was disposed of as having been irreparably damaged by water and rats. Speculation abounds that the suitcase may have contained a revised version of Benjamin's *Passagenwerk* — his extraordinarily detailed and fragmented account of the commercial arcade passages of nineteenth-century Paris. Aside from this tentative linking of the two towns' respective fortunes, this speculation also suggests another irony around the idea of passage — Portbou's belated acknowledgement of Benjamin's thwarted passage through it, right at the moment when its own interstitial significance is about to largely disappear.

I keep coming back to the heavily pixelated shot of Portbou on Google Maps that was my first visual encounter with the town — how it was tempting to read the blocky pixels, showing the railway sidings as so much blurred scar tissue, not as a temporary technological aberration but as a kind of deliberate satellite indifference reflecting the town's coming 'irrelevance' — a casually violent dismissal of its future. A future of occasional drivers slowing by the tourist booth corner with no intention of stopping, in a town built on stopping.

And thinking about this satellite observing the town, I thought too of Benjamin's own description of Paul Klee's *Angelus Novus*, in which he describes that image as 'the angel of history. His face is turned towards the past. Where we perceive a chain of events, he sees one single catastrophe which keeps piling wreckage upon wreckage.' It made me want to record some details of this slowing town whilst the satellite angels marked more urgent velocities elsewhere.

THE PHOTO ESSAY *Narrow Gauge* was shot in Portbou on July 24, 2007. Each 48" x 36" image contains a digital watermark in the form of a small-print fragment of spam e-mail embedded in the lower left corner of the composition. The message from which this text was taken would have been received in a 'prepared' inbox (a webmail address left deliberately exposed to spam address trawlers) at the same time as the corresponding photo was taken and adds a kind of inadvertent temporal metadata to the image. The text also exists at such a scale as to compromise the integrity of the larger image, were a viewer to attempt to move from looking at the largely consistent surface of the picture as a whole to reading this tiny embedded fragment. To make such a shift from viewing to reading would involve moving so physically close to the image that the whole scene would be impossible for the eye to maintain, even without the now-obvious pixelation and paper grain that this new level of scrutiny would reveal.

Narrow Gauge is not *about* Portbou or the railway yards, Walter Benjamin or locative media, even if it couldn't exist without any of these phenomena and in different ways features traces and knowledge of all of them. If it's about anything, it's about spam. Something of spam's use of the very qualities of the electronic network itself within its attempted acts of forestalling and the thought that this prompts of filtered passages through mountains. Something of the way that the atavistic urge that drives spam's adaptive activity has historically found ways to make the leap from transport paradigm to transport paradigm, even as technologies and their housings become obsolete — suggesting that spam takes its place in a long line of delinquent readings of transport potential. There's something here too about spam's ability to move with very little friction wherever information goes and to carry no sentiment about where it's been or what it leaves in its wake — this lowest common denominator chatter on the wires of global economic power and desire in motion. A chatter that speaks to the fact that the con is always with us wherever uncritical claims of progress are made.

PORTBOU

ORTA DE LA COSTA BRAVA

W. Benjamin

Walter Benjamin

El pas d'una frontera

Walter Benjamin, disposava d'un salconduit per poder travessar Espanya i dirigir-se a Lisboa, on pensava embarcar-se cap els Estats Units. En el seu pensament, la idea d'haver sortit del malson de la persecució nazi i de saber que era lliure, el va portar a presentar-se a les autoritats espanyoles per regularitzar la seva situació. Al llarg de la seva vida, ja des de la infantesa, Benjamin s'havia sentit acompanyat d'una mena de malastrugança –l'anomenava el geperut, un personatge dels comptes alemanys–. A la comissaria de policia, Benjamin rep la notícia de la denegació del permís d'entrada a Espanya. Li cal disposar d'una autorització per sortir de França. Excepcionalment i pel seu estat de salut se li permet quedar-se a fer nit a Portbou. La policia l'acompanya, juntament amb Henny Gurland i Joseph, a la Fonda França.

Walter Benjamin disponía de un salvoconducto para poder atravesar España y dirigirse a Lisboa, desde donde pensaba embarcarse hacia los Estados Unidos. En su pensamiento, la idea de haber podido escapar a la pesadilla de la persecución nazi y de saber que era libre le llevó a presentarse ante las autoridades españolas para regularizar su situación. A lo largo de su vida, ya desde su infancia, Benjamin se había sentido acompañado por una especie de desdicha –la denominaba el jorobado– un personaje de los cuentos alemanes. En la comisaría de policía, Benjamin recibe la noticia de que le ha sido denegado su permiso de entrada en España. Precisa de una autorización para poder salir de Francia. Excepcionalmente, y debido a su estado de salud, se le permite pernoctar en Portbou. La policía le acompaña, juntamente con Henny Gurland y Joseph, a la Fonda França.

Walter Benjamin disposait d'un sauf-conduit afin de pouvoir traverser l'Espagne et se diriger à Lisbonne où il avait l'intention d'embarquer pour les États-Unis. Dans son esprit, l'idée d'être sorti du cauchemar de la persécution nazie et de se savoir libre le poussa à se présenter auprès des autorités espagnoles pour régulariser sa situation. Sa vie durant, et déjà dans son enfance, Benjamin avait eu la sensation d'être poursuivi par la malchance – qu'il appelait le bossu, un personnage des contes allemands. Au commissariat, Benjamin reçoit la nouvelle du refus du permis d'entrée en Espagne ; il doit disposer d'une autorisation pour quitter la France. Exceptionnellement, et en raison de son état de santé, il lui est permis de passer la nuit à Portbou. La police l'accompagne, avec Henny Gurland et Joseph, à la Fonda França.

Walter B[...] to cross S[...] he thoug[...] States. T[...] escaping [...] and know[...] to the S[...] situation [...] he was a [...] dogged [...] 'hunchb[...] folklore [...] At the p[...] his perm[...] He neede[...] Exceptio[...] was allow[...] The polic[...] Henny G[...] known a[...]

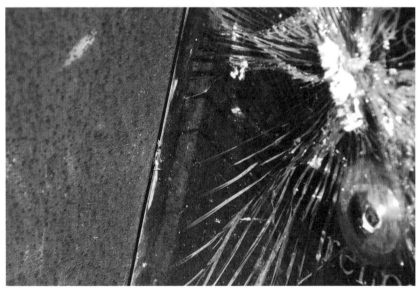

Portbou, 1940

ILLUSTRATIONS

FRONT AND BACK COVER *Cacklebladder*, Graham Parker, 2006. From a series of neon signs based on titles of spam e-mails.

INSIDE FRONT COVER *Untitled (bullethole on memorial)* (detail), Graham Parker, Giclée print, 2007.

INSIDE BACK COVER *Untitled (street sign)* (detail), Graham Parker, Giclée print, 2007.

PAGES 1 AND 6 Graphic at start and end of the text is the Portbou town emblem.

PAGE 24 Hand-drawn diagram of Portbou railway sidings based on existing map and observation, Graham Parker, 2007.

All other images untitled, from photo series *Narrow Gauge*. Giclée prints. Dimensions 48" x 34" unless otherwise stated. © Graham Parker, 2007.

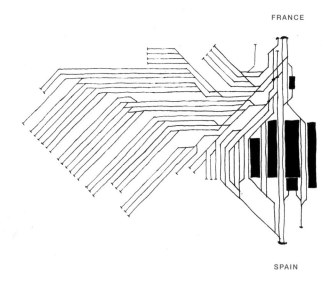

FRANCE

SPAIN